Maſſaw-Omecks

Maſſawomeck

VIA

HONI SOIT QVI MALY PENSE

Significa...
To the cro...
what beyond...

Kings hou...

Ordinary h...

Tanxfnitama

ACKS

N

Pamacocack

Tauxenent

Namaſſingakent

Aſſaomeck

Namorauahquend

Cepowig

Teſſamatuck

Woſameus

Nacotchtanck

Mattpanient

Quactataugh

cliffes

The Saſques-ahanou
are a Gyant like peo=ple &
Vtchowig thus a tyred

S A S Q V

Attaock

Teſingh

L H A N

Quadroque

O V G H

K    BAY

Powels Iles

Bines poynt

Small poynt

W.flowbres flu:

Smyths Iles

Saſquefahanough

A t...

Ozinies

Poynt Peſmae

Kulacawack

Tockwogh flu:

Acquaina...

WA
KS

T O C K

W O G H S

Peregryns mount

A N A C...

and halſe

ues

Leagues

Chickahokin

Macocks

H V K...

5        10        15

...ered and Diſcribed by Captayn John Smith
Grauen by William Hole

# Historic
# Virginia

This book was devised and produced by
Multimedia Publications (UK) Ltd.

**Editor: Marilyn Inglis**
**Production: Arnon Orbach**
**Design: Behram Kapadia**
**Picture Research: Virginia Landry &**
**Charlotte Deane**

First published in the United States of
America 1985 by Gallery Books, an imprint of
W. H. Smith Publishers Inc., 112 Madison
Avenue, New York, NY 10016

ISBN 0 8317 4207 0

Origination by Imago
Printed in Italy by Sagdos, Milan
Typesetting by Flowery Typesetters Ltd

# Historic Virginia

## Brian Beckett

GALLERY BOOKS
An Imprint of W. H. Smith Publishers Inc.
112 Madison Avenue
New York City 10016

# CONTENTS

1 Cradle of the Nation 6

2 Origins 14

3 Revolution 24

4 The Civil War 34

5 Seeing the Sights 42

6 Modern Days 54

# CHAPTER 1

# Cradle of the Nation

Virginia, the "Old Dominion", was the first English colony in North America, and in many ways modern American history started here. From Jamestown, where the first permanent colony of hardy pioneers established itself, to Appomattox, where the Civil War ended, Virginia is a living history book. Yorktown, Fredericksburg, Chancellorsville and Petersburg are battlefields which decided America's destiny. Reconstructions of colonial buildings in Jamestown, Yorktown and – especially – Williamsburg are world renowned. Scattered across Virginia are the gracious stately homes from the age of the great plantations.

In addition to George Washington's Mount Vernon, the Lee House overlooking Arlington Cemetery, and the Byrds' Belle Air, there are dozens of others – many perfectly preserved – unknown to the average American. But there are also simpler homes equally worth seeing. Twenty miles south of Roanoke in southwest Virginia is the cabin where the black leader Booker T. Washington was born in slavery and also a reconstruction of the tobacco plantation he worked on as a child.

Virginia has been called the "Mother of Presidents". Four of the first five Presidents were Virginian: George Washington, Thomas Jefferson, James Madison and James Monroe. Four more Virginians were also to become President: William Henry Harrison (the ninth), John Tyler (the tenth), Zachary Taylor (the twelfth), and Woodrow Wilson (the twenty-eighth).

*Left* The Governor's Palace, Williamsburg, the home of seven British Governors and of Patrick Henry and Thomas Jefferson. One of the most elegant mansions of colonial America, it is surrounded by a large formal garden.

*Above* Tobacco drying in a barn in Grayson County. Before Columbus arrived, tobacco was cultivated and used by the Indians all over the Americas. It was not long before Europeans carried the habit to the Old World. In 1613 John Rolfe, who married Pocahontas, crossed imported West Indian seeds with local Indian tobacco and produced a smoke which soon became enormously popular and profitable. Despite King James I's dislike of the noxious weed, Virginia was soon exporting 50 000 pounds' weight of the crop to Britain. This was the beginning of booming prosperity for Virginia and was an important factor in the survival of the young colony.

*Right* The glowing colors of fall foliage in Virginia almost rivals New England's more famous display. Virginians whose lives have taken them to the big cities fondly remember sights like this.

*Above* Gathering in the harvest near Richmond. Although more than half of all Virginians now live in cities, and industry and government are essential to the economy of Virginia, agriculture is still a vital mainstay.

Other famous Virginians are household names: Washington, Robert E. Lee and "Stonewall" Jackson are among America's greatest generals. In more recent times, Generals Douglas MacArthur, George Catlett Marshall and George Smith Patton had links with the state. In the political arena, George Mason, Richard Henry Lee and Patrick Henry were in the forefront of America's rebellion against the British. Patrick Henry is best remembered for his passionate "give me liberty, or give me death" speech to the Virginia Convention but, after arguing against the Federal Constitution (because he thought it a danger to liberty), he also become famous as a political good loser. Modern Virginians often display an understandable pride in these distinguished fellow-Virginians.

There are also Virginians whose names are less familiar, but who should be famous: Generals Winfield Scott and George Thomas, for instance, who remained loyal to the Union after secession. Thomas is considered by many to have been one of the Union's most brilliant officers, but he was largely forgotten after the war.

History lives in Virginia. America's longest-running quarrel dates back to 1632 when King Charles I gouged Maryland out of north Virginia to give to his friend Lord Baltimore. He gave him "the further bank" of the Potomac as the southern boundary, so giving him the river and denying Virginia's crab and oyster fishermen (whose products still grace restaurant tables throughout the Eastern Seaboard) valuable fishing grounds. The two states have been arguing about this ever since the so-called "oyster war", and fishermen were killed over it.

Even if it wanted to, Virginia could not throw off the legacy of its past; its roots are so deep and its life so tenacious.

*Above* Just a few of the many different types of traditional craftsmen working in Williamsburg, these coopers (barrel makers) are trussing a barrel – putting the hoops around the staves.

*Right* Surrender Field, Yorktown, where the American victory brought the Revolution to a successful end after a siege of almost three months. An annual Yorktown event, with parades and other ceremonies, commemorates the surrender of the British General Cornwallis.

*Above* America's past is remembered with colorful pageantry – and music!

*Above* A dramatic picture of the Rebel Yell, one of the most exciting of the dozens of thrill rides at King's Dominion.

*Left* A colorful and friendly scene at exciting King's Dominion, the Disneyland of Virginia, with 800 acres of amusement for all the family.

*Right* A favorite pastime at Virginia Beach, famous for a warm summer that lasts from April through October. The fishing opportunities here include channel bass, spot, flounder, croaker, pickerel, perch and whiting. There is an annual Virginia Salt Water Fishing Tournament from May through November.

# CHAPTER 2

# *Origins*

For a while Virginia was America. In 1587 – some 33 years before the *Mayflower* sailed – Sir Walter Raleigh sent 117 men, women and children to settle in the hostile wilderness that was to become the Eastern Seaboard of the United States. Earlier reports had told him of a fertile land populated by Indians "void of all guile" living "after the manner of the golden age". Raleigh was one of Queen Elizabeth's favorites, and she allowed him to name his colony after her own nickname, the "virgin queen".

The hardy pioneers put ashore on Roanoke Island off the coast of what is now North Carolina ("Virginia" then meant all the land stretching from the Atlantic coast to the Mississippi River). It was a risky time to found a colony: England's sea captains were more interested in plundering Spanish gold further south, and Elizabeth's government was preparing to deal with the Spaniards – the Armada was not defeated until 1588. It was another two years before other ships sent by Raleigh reached Virginia, and when the crew finally landed the ill-fated colonists had vanished without a trace. What happened to them is still a mystery.

This was England's second failure (an earlier Raleigh hundred-man expedition to Roanoke Island in 1585 had to be

*Left* It was small ships like these that brought the first intrepid colonists to Jamestown in 1607 after a hazardous journey of 18 long weeks at sea. These replicas are to be found on the James River.

*Inset* Queen Elizabeth I, and her favorite courtier, Sir Walter Raleigh, whom she encouraged in his exploits across the Atlantic.

Within the illustration:
*Their rype corne*
*Their greene corne.*
*Corne newly sprong.*
*Their sitting at meate*
*The place of Solemne prayer*
*The howse wherin the Tombe of their Herounds standeth.*
SECOTON·
*A Ceremony in their prayers w strange testures and songes danssig abowt posts carued on the toppes lyke mens faces.*

*Above* John White's watercolor of the Indian village of Secoton, painted in 1587. White was in Raleigh's 1585 colony in Roanoke, which was rescued by Sir Francis Drake, and he illustrated the first careful description of North American Indians written by an Englishman (Thomas Hariot).

120 colonists boarded three tiny ships, *Susan Constant* (100 tons), *Godspeed* (40 tons), and *Discovery* (20 tons), and sailed from London for a new life across the sea. After 18 arduous weeks at sea they reached Chesapeake Bay, and on May 14, 1607 the settlers put ashore on a low-lying swampy peninsula at what is now Jamestown, named after the king.

Standing in Jamestown today, with its relaxed atmosphere and modern comforts, it is hard to picture the misery and grueling hardships of those first days in that unhealthy, marshy place. In the first six months, half the colonists died and the rest faced death from starvation and hostile Indian tribes. By the new year, though, a ship from England brought much-needed supplies, and an alliance of sorts had been formed with the Indian chief Powhatan, thanks to Captain John Smith's friendship with Pocahontas, the chief's daughter.

Later, as the bride of colonist John Rolfe, the captivating Pocahontas was to sail to London and, dressed in Elizabethan finery, she became America's first goodwill ambassador to the Court of St James. Sadly, she died shortly after. Today, the Jamestown Festival Park contains not only full-scale replicas of the three small ships that carried the first Jamestown settlers but reproductions of the kind of Indian lodge, with its stone-age tools, lived in by Pocahontas and her tribe. From stone-age lodge to Elizabethan finery, Pocahontas indeed had a unique life!

Travel through Virginia's farmlands today and you'll find its most historic product – tobacco. In 1613, John Rolfe crossed West Indian tobacco with native Virginian products: the result was a smoke that took England by storm and a blossoming colonial economy. Goods were bought and sold for tobacco, and new colonists who arrived penniless were soon able to return home with small fortunes. Crops were even grown in Jamestown's streets, and a minority of the wealthier Virginia Company shareholders were able to form a cartel which kept the colony supplied with the basic necessities of life in exchange for a monopoly on the selling of tobacco in England. By 1620 the Company was recruiting English women and shipping them to Jamestown and the fee was 150 pounds of tobacco for a wife.

For years, though, the colonists' hold on Virginia was precarious. In 1622 Pocahontas' uncle, Opechancanough, who followed Powhatan as chief, saw the growing threat to the Indian's way of life, broke the fragile alliance, and launched a

rescued by Sir Francis Drake), but in 1606 the new King James I granted a charter to the Virginia Company to try again. Shares of Virginia Company common stock cost £2. 10s each, and there were many small investors. Shortly before Christmas 1606,

sudden attack which wiped out nearly a third of the Virginia colony just as it was beginning to take firm root. In the political skirmishing that followed, the Virginia Company's Charter was withdrawn and the territory became a Crown Colony.

Virginia now began an era of blossoming prosperity – by 1650 the population had grown to some 15 000. Tragically, this figure included a few hundred black slaves – the seeds of future conflict. By 1670, Virginia's population reached about 40 000, but Pocahontas' people numbered only a few thousand, as the Indian population dwindled.

Large tracts of land were granted to settlers willing to pay for the transport of at least 250 people. These grants were self-governing and were known as "hundreds" or "plantations". This was the beginnings of the famous plantation system which produced the stately homes scattered across Virginia today.

Visitors to Norfolk shouldn't miss seeing America's oldest brick house, built by Adam Thoroughgood in 1636. As a boy Thoroughgood began his career as a servant in Virginia, but he prospered and returned to England and brought back a wife and family and nearly 40 servants. He encouraged the transport of other settlers (which was very profitable to him) and in a few years his estate covered over 5000 acres.

In the 1650s, an English sailor liked the look of Virginia and decided to settle. His name was John Washington and in about ten years he had acquired more than 5000 acres, including Wakefield, the birthplace of his renowned descendant. Wakefield burned down on Christmas Day 1779, but the National Park Service has built a full reproduction from old brick and other original materials.

By the late 1660s, Virginia was again suffering hard times due to high taxes and a collapse in the price of tobacco. In 1675, friction with local Indian tribes verged on all-out war. Nathaniel Bacon, a gentle-born English ne'er-do-well who had been expelled from Cambridge and sent to Virginia for a new start, led a brief rebellion against the colonial governor, came perilously close to success, and captured the imagination of the general population. Nevertheless, the colony was there to stay, part of a thriving cluster of English settlements covering eastern North America.

By the 1680s, Virginia's population had reached over 70 000. Some 3000 were black, but a large number of these were freed slaves who had invested in land and become fairly wealthy. Several of

*Above* A colored engraving of Pocahontas saving the life of Captain John Smith. Captain Smith was captured by the Indians and condemned to death, and, according to his story, was rescued by Pocahontas, daughter of Chief Powhatan. It was partly Captain Smith's friendship with the Indian Princess that saved the colony in the early miserably hard years, menaced by disease, starvation and hostile Indians.

*Left* The Indian Princess Pocahontas, who Captain John Smith, in his *Generall Historie of Virginia,* said saved his life by cradling his head in her arms to stop Powhatan's braves from clubbing him to death. She later later married John Rolfe, and accompanied him to England. She died while preparing to return to America.

Virginia's richer landed black people entered the African slave trade in their own right, and with the profits imported servants from England in the tradition of white settlers. Virginia's free black community arose from slaves freed as a reward for service, or by owners who didn't believe in slavery, or – at least in some cases – after their conversion to Christianity. In 1670, though, the Virginia Assembly passed laws against black people owning white servants and making it clear that a man's slavery was not altered by his baptism. Within a decade or so, the institution of slavery was firmly rooted in Virginia.

Virginia had now come of age: the middle-class captains of commerce continued to build their fortunes and their magnificent homes – Carter's Grove, for example, some six miles southeast of Williamsburg on US Route 60, was built in 1750 by Robert "King" Carter, one of the wealthiest men in early America. His fortune was built on a large inheritance from his father John, who had made a fortune from tobacco and from a happy knack of marrying rich women – he had five wives who brought him more and more land.

For decades England's children had maintained a precarious grip on Virginia's coast, and very gradually began to move inland: soon they would spread westward in what was to become a flood. In the very southwest corner of Virginia there is the Cumberland Gap through the Allegheny Mountains: it was discovered in 1750, and explored by Daniel Boone as America stood on the brink of revolution just over two decades later. By the revolution's end something like 12 000 settlers had passed through the Alleghenies along Boone's Wilderness Road into what is now Kentucky. Nine years later the population was 100 000 and Kentucky was a state of the new Union. Today you can drive the same route and visit the Cumberland Gap National Park which covers some 32

*Above* A reconstruction of the original settlers' fort built in Jamestown for protection against the Indians in 1607.

*Right* Cannons fire once again in Williamsburg, which once held the arsenal of colonial Virginia. Demonstrations of the use of early guns are often given.

*Left* A drum and fife corps play the traditional stirring music as part of the loving recreation of the past in Williamsburg.

19

square miles and contains some of the most beautiful scenery in America.

Despite the appalling early hardships and uncertainties, when Jamestown was a crude fortified trading post and Virginia's first citizens little more than employees of stockholders in England, faith and vision kept a doubtful enterprise alive. In 1610, when things were at their worst, Virginia's governor sent a report to London which soon found itself partly put into poetry:

> *Be not dismayed at all*
> *For scandal cannot do us wrong,*
> *God will not let us fall . . .*
> *For that our work is good;*
> *We hope to plant a nation*
> *Where none before hath stood.*

It was a spirit akin to this which opened up the West and made the nation great.

*Facing page, top* The Governor's Palace, Williamsburg, at the north end of Palace Green, was the residence of British Governors and the first two Governors of the Commonwealth of Virginia, Patrick Henry and Thomas Jefferson. A stately public building, it combines dignity and restraint with an aristocratic awareness of its worth in the familiar eighteenth-century manner. The original building was burnt down in 1781. The present-day reconstruction is furnished with valuable antiques, and the building is surrounded by a 10-acre garden, complete with a maze and a canal. Among the several out-buildings is a stable, where you can watch a wheelwright in action.

*Facing page, bottom* A quiet scene in Williamsburg. The city was once the political, social and cultural center of America. It became the seat of government in 1699 and remained so until the capital was shifted to Richmond. After that it became a quiet college town of great charm. It now has the largest number of reconstructed eighteenth-century buildings in America. In 1927 John D. Rockefeller initiated the funding, and today, after over $90 million and much devoted labor have been lavished on it, the restoration and reconstructions cover an area of about a mile by a half-mile.

*Right* The inside of a house in Jamestown, site of the earliest colony in Virginia. Jamestown has many reminders of the early days of America for the visitor to see, including the fort, the Old Church Tower, the Old World Pavilion, and Powhatan's Lodge, a reconstruction of an Indian chief's dwelling.

*Above* Part of Jamestown Festival Park's reconstruction in wattle and daub of the original 1607 settlement in Jamestown. There are a few dozen of these quaint buildings, among which are dwelling houses, a church and a gatehouse. During the summer, guides dressed in the colorful costume of seventeenth-century halberdiers, complete with crimson sash and stockings, will explain the exhibits.

*Left* Daniel Boone played a vital part in opening up the route to the West. Just after the French and Indian War, Boone and other "long hunters" explored the Appalachians through to Kentucky and brought back reports of fertile land and huge herds of buffalo and deer. Soon after, thousands of people were to pour through the Cumberland Gap, following the Wilderness Road blazed by Boone and 30 axemen in 1775. In the late eighteenth- and early nineteenth-centuries, something like 200 000 settlers used the pass. From there civilization was to spread right across the West to the Pacific.

*Above* The ancient art of barrel making
flourishes in Williamsburg, where you can
watch the fascinating craft being practised.

*Right* One of the delights of historic
Williamsburg, and a fine old-fashioned way to
see the town – by relaxing on a tranquil
carriage tour. You can take a ride through the
historic part of Williamsburg in a carriage
driven by a coachman in full traditional
costume. The tours themselves are booked in
the 1770 Courthouse.

# *Revolution*

In the midst of the bustle of modern Williamsburg, there is the reconstructed Raleigh tavern (Duke of Gloucester St) complete with original eighteenth-century furnishings. In 1774, the British blockaded Boston in reprisal for the recent "Tea Party". Relief supplies flowed in from the other colonies and, in May, the Virginia Assembly passed a Resolve talking of "hostile invasion". The Assembly was quickly dissolved by the governor, but its members retired to the Raleigh tavern, where they spoke of an attack on "all America" and drafted letters to similar bodies in other colonies suggesting a Continental Congress. It met in Philadelphia in September and among other things published a Declaration of Rights insisting on the rights of English law in the colonies.

As pressure for separation grew, another "unofficial" meeting of Virginia's burghers in Williamsburg appointed a committee to draw up a Bill of Rights (which became the model for all American bills of rights) and voted to order its Congressional delegation to support full American independence. In June 1776, the Congress told a five-man committee headed by Jefferson to draft a Declaration of Independence. After a few weeks of quibbling, their draft was adopted on July 4, 1776. The American Revolution was probably inevitable, but much of the credit for getting things going belongs to some far-sighted men meeting in a Williamsburg tavern.

If you visit the small and quiet coastal city of Yorktown, have a look at the stately

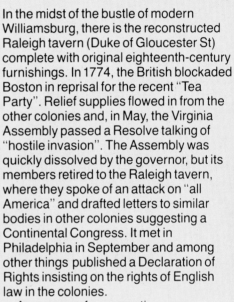

*Left* The surrender at Yorktown, painted by Van Blarenberghe (1716-94).
*Inset* Yorktown battlefield, part of Colonial National Historical Park. It displays the remains of the British fortifications as well as parts of the French and American camps.

home of Governor Thomas Nelson. It's still a marvelous example of colonial architecture, but embedded in a wall are some eighteenth-century cannonballs. In October 1781 the British General Cornwallis found himself bottled up here. To the west was Washington's revolutionary army and, in the seas behind him, the French fleet. For three weeks, Washington's bedraggled troops besieged the town. As one of Washington's serving officers, Nelson noticed that the American artillery was taking pains not to hit his home, which was being used by the British command. Nelson stepped forward and ordered the gunners to fire on his house.

America's war had been going on for nearly five years before Cornwallis found his way to Yorktown. Since 1776, George III's regulars and his German mercenaries had fought Washington's Continental Army without a clear result. Britain held America's chief cities, but could not win a decisive battle against a rebel army which was poorly supplied and riddled with personal rivalries. The war ranged from New England, where the farmers first fired the "shot heard around the world", to the Carolinas, where the British fought a bloody but indecisive war. One of Washington's officers, "Light Horse Harry" Lee, was already renowned as the leader of an elite cavalry legion famed for its discipline and skill. It was "Light Horse Harry" Lee who later immortalized Washington as "First in war, first in peace, first in the hearts of his countrymen," but his son was soon to find far greater fame in a wider and bloodier war: his name was Robert E. Lee.

Cornwallis' Carolinas campaign ended in March 1781 at the Battle of Guilford Courthouse, where the British won the day but with such casualties and extended supply lines that they were still forced to fall back. Under renewed American pressure, Cornwallis soon found himself retreating to Wilmington, but even on the very day of the Guilford battle, Cornwallis had found a grander strategy: he could win the war in Virginia. "If we mean an offensive war in America," he wrote, "we must abandon New York" – the main British garrison – "and bring our whole force into Virginia; we then have a stake to fight for, and a successful battle may give us America."

New York stayed British but in April Cornwallis was allowed to leave for Virginia, where Benedict Arnold – now one of King George's generals – had been campaigning since January. Cornwallis marched to Petersburg, Virginia, where

*Above* George Washington. Called from retirement to command the Continental armies, Washington's tenacity and self-control eventually forced Cornwallis' surrender.

*Right* The Kitchen House at George Washington Birthplace National Monument at Wakefield, the site of Popes Creek Plantation, the birthplace and early home of George Washington, the first President.

*Below* A wider view of Popes Creek Plantation (Wakefield), where George Washington was born to fairly well-to-do parents on the fringes of the upper class. Wakefield is now a working colonial farm. Washington was later devoted to Mount Vernon, adding to the house and working to improve the estate.

he met with reinforcements sent from New York. His total forces numbered just over 7000 and, after a few sorties as far as Charlottesville (one nearly captured Thomas Jefferson), Cornwallis marched his men to Yorktown. Here he hoped to stake out an impregnable position with a sea-front linking his army to the warships of the British Navy.

The siege of Yorktown began on September 28, a fortnight after the French had won a decisive sea battle, and on October 19 Cornwallis sent out his deputy to make a formal surrender. Lines of American and French soldiers taunted British troops as they gave up their arms, and military bands played *The World Turned Upside Down*. The war was over, but it took another year of wrangling between all the warring parties before a formal treaty was signed giving the 13 colonies their independence.

Visitors to Yorktown should drop in at the National Parks Service's Visitor Center and see a short film plus numerous exhibits showing just what happened from the day Cornwallis' troops marched into Yorktown to his surrender three months later. Markers are scattered throughout the town showing just where various highlights of the battle took place. Other documentary films tell the story of the entire Revolutionary War. Yorktown's civic pride is understandable; Washington won the battle and America won the war.

NICOLSON'S SHOP

*Facing page top* A French grand battery at Yorktown. When France entered the War of Independence on the side of the rebels, the outcome was really decided. The French fleet played an important part in bringing about the surrender at Yorktown, and their troops helped in the siege.

*Facing page, bottom* The vivid scene of preparations to fire antique rifles on Market Square Green, Williamsburg, as part of the town's continued recreation of the past.

*Above* Nicolson's shop, Williamsburg, one of the many shops in recreated Williamsburg which give the flavor of life in the colonial town.

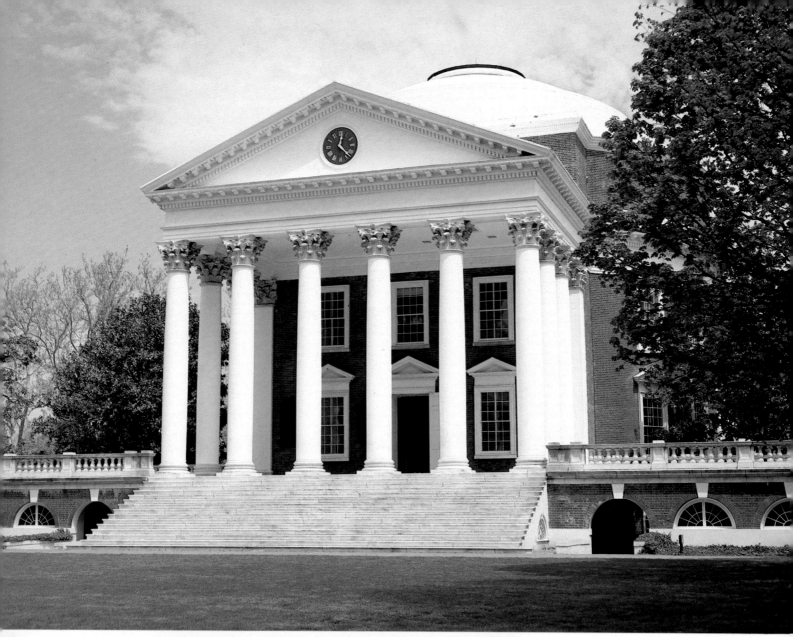

*Above* The Rotunda, University of Virginia, designed by Thomas Jefferson. He was instrumental in founding the University and he designed its buildings. This rotunda was based on the Roman Pantheon.

*Left* Monticello, Thomas Jefferson's home, not far from the University of Virginia, just outside Charlottesville. The furnishings include many of his ingenious contrivances.

*Above* Thomas Jefferson's Monticello. An elegant mansion on the side of a mountain with a Blue Ridge background, Monticello took about 12 years to build, though Jefferson was never wholly satisfied with it. As a student of architecture, Jefferson much admired classical models, and Monticello became something like a Roman villa.

*Right* Thomas Jefferson, painted by Rembrandt Peale in 1800. Jefferson was one of America's most distinguished men, third President of the United States, and man of many talents – lawyer, politician, statesman, ambassador, inventor, architect, writer. Present when Patrick Henry made his famous "Give me liberty, or give me death" speech, Jefferson wrote the inspiring Declaration of Independence.

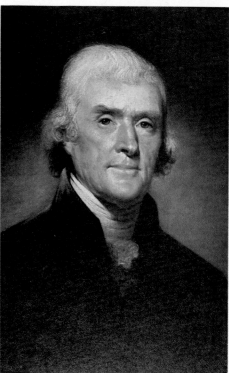

*Right* Nightlife on King Street, Alexandria. In the eighteenth-century a political and cultural center, Alexandria, across the Potomac from Washington DC, is now a center of science, commerce, transportation and trade.

*Below* Proud of its past, Alexandria has restored and cared for many of its old buildings. It has a charmingly restored eighteenth-century neighborhood, Old Town Alexandria, founded by Scottish merchants in colonial times. One of the easiest ways to get to know it is to take a conducted walking tour of historic sites.

*Facing page* A fascinating blend of old and new, Alexandria has something to satisfy everyone.

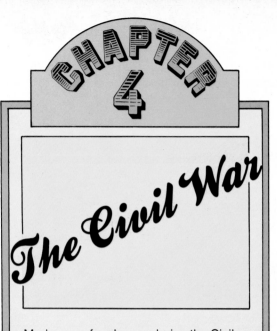

# CHAPTER 4

# The Civil War

Modern warfare began during the Civil War, much of which took place in Virginia, as the advanced front of the Confederacy. Sixty years before the bitter carnage of World War I, Union and Confederate armies faced each other across trenches outside Petersburg, south of Richmond. In March 1862, the Confederate man-of-war *Virginia* (formerly the *Merrimack*) fought the USS *Monitor* in the world's first sea battle between iron-clad warships. Two years later the Confederate RL *Huntley* became the first submarine in history to sink another warship. Naval mines, the telegraph and railways became instruments of war for the first time. Observation balloons had been used before, but came of age during the Civil War. (One Union balloonist over Chancellorsville, Virginia, reported Confederate Stonewall Jackson's cavalry moving off in a flanking attack: unfortunately for the Union, the information was ignored and Lee won one of his greatest victories.)

More Americans lost their lives in the Civil War than in World Wars I and II put together. The destruction of Virginia's territory was horrendous, and some 15 000 of her sons died.

Of all the Confederate states, only Virginia hesitated over secession after Lincoln's election in 1860 – it didn't leave the Union until April 1861. The counties of northwest Virginia beyond the Appalachians had considerable Union sentiment, and they then seceded from Virginia to become the state of West Virginia. Colonel Robert E. Lee had little

A potent and sinister symbol of warfare in Manassas National Park.

*Right* Arlington National Cemetery, America's largest and most famous cemetery, once part of the plantation home of Robert E. Lee, and his wife Mary Custis, great granddaughter of Martha Washington. Taken over by the Union during the Civil War and used as a military camp, part of the estate was set aside for a national cemetery. Among the illustrious dead here are President John F. Kennedy, Senator Robert F. Kennedy and Oliver Wendell Holmes. Honoring the unsung dead is the Tomb of the Unknown Soldier.

*Top left* During the battle of Fredericksburg, dominated by the Confederacy under Robert E. Lee, Union troops under General Ambrose Burnside repeatedly charged one of the strongest enemy postions of the entire Civil War – the "terrible stone wall." Total losses were 12 653 for the Union, 5903 for the Confederacy. The site of the battle is now part of Fredericksburg and Spotsylvania National Military Park.

*Bottom left* No clear decision emerged from the battle between the USS *Monitor* and the Confederate *Virginia* (ex-*Merrimack*) in the battle of Hampton Roads. This was the world's first sea battle between two armor-clad ships, but it took place too late to influence the Peninsula Campaign. The Confederacy was at a naval disadvantage throughout the war.

sympathy himself with slavery and none with secession. "Secession", he wrote to his family, "is nothing but revolution . . . still a union that can only be maintained by swords and bayonets . . . has no charm for me." He turned down the command of the US Army, resigned his commission, and returned to Virginia to "share the miseries of my people."

The war ended in Virginia with Lee's surrender at Appomattox, and in a real sense it also began in Virginia, when the abolitionist John Brown raided the Federal arsenal at Harper's Ferry (now in West Virginia) in October 1859. He was captured a few days later by militia and

Federal troops (led by Colonel Robert E. Lee) and he was hanged on December 2, 1859, but his actions frightened pro-slavery Southerners and made secession far more attractive. Visitors to West Virginia may relive Brown's private war in the Harper's Ferry National Historic Park.

In the first weeks of the war, the popular cry in the North was "On to Richmond!" and everybody hoped for a short war. In July 1861, Lincoln sent the Union Army across the Potomac into Virginia to meet the Confederate forces at Manassas Junction in front of day-tripping socialites from Washington, DC. Better known as "Bull Run", the battle went to the South,

and during it General Thomas "Stonewall" Jackson got his nickname.

In early 1862, General George McClellan, commanding the Union's Army of the Potomac, planned a quick attack on Richmond, but found that the Confederates had garrisoned the city of Fredericksburg and barred his path. He opted for a flanking attack, and at the end of March landed on the York Peninsula, where he hoped to move up on Richmond from below. He might have done it, but he wasted time laying siege to a small Confederate force in Yorktown.

Lee used the time to build his army, and when the Confederates abandoned

Yorktown, McClellan had to fight his way through Williamsburg, where in June/July he met Lee and Jackson in the Seven Days' Battle, including the blood-letting at Malvern Hill with over 35 000 casualties. Shortly afterwards, the Union Army began a partial withdrawal and the Confederacy looked safe from conquest.

To keep independence, the Confederacy had only to defend itself as well as it had just done, but Lee decided to hurry things along by invading Pennsylvania to cut the Union in two: he was soundly defeated at Antietam on September 17, 1862. Just over a month later, the Army of the Potomac under its new commander, General Ambrose Burnside, met Lee's forces at Fredericksburg, and there, in what is now a national park of pleasant rural countryside, occurred one of the bloodiest slaughters of the war, as wave after wave of Union troops charged across open ground towards Lee's entrenched positions on Maryes Heights, only to be mowed down by cannonfire and sharpshooters from behind a stone wall.

The following May (1863) Lee met the Army of the Potomac under yet another new commander, General Joseph Hooker, at Chancellorsville, west of Fredericksburg. He sent Stonewall Jackson on a surprise flanking attack, and with the Union Army (almost twice the size of Lee's!) on the brink of defeat, Hooker retreated. The South's victory cost them dearly, though: Stonewall Jackson was mistakenly shot by his own men and died a week later, depriving the South of one of its most brilliant commanders. His last words were "Let us cross over the river and rest under the shade of the trees."

Flushed with success, Lee invaded Pennsylvania again, and on July 1, he met General George Meade in a three-day battle at Gettysburg. Lee was forced to withdraw, and within a few months the Union's General Sherman began the drive eastward which would take him into Atlanta just over a year later. By then, Grant (General-in-Chief of the Union Armies from March 1864) was again driving on Richmond, and in May he found himself fighting a five-day battle at Spotsylvania. Here a terrible period of trench warfare began as Grant repeatedly tried without success to break the Confederate lines. Grant then moved on to Petersburg, but yet again found himself facing an entrenched Lee. Union assaults on Petersburg cost some 8000 casualties in just four days.

As would happen again in 1914, two

*Facing page, top* General Burnside commanded the Army of the Potomac at the disastrous (for the Union) battle of Fredericksburg. Previously a competent commander at a lower level of responsibility, trained at West Point and a veteran of the Mexican War, his incompetence at Fredericksburg came as an unpleasant shock to the Union, and he was relieved of his command. After further reverses, he eventually resigned his commission.

*Facing page, bottom* During the whole of the Civil War the Union was better equipped in artillery and munitions than the South. The Union artillery was mostly muzzle-loading, using the "Napoleon" or the Parrott cannon. The Southern artillery was an assemblage of imported or captured weaponry.

*Above* The tranquillity of the Shenandoah Valley was brutally shattered by the necessities of the Civil War. Stonewall Jackson fought a brilliant campaign here, and in the best-remembered battle in the valley – New Market – 247 VMI cadets forged a legend.

*Right* Scenics Mill, Beaver Dam. In 1864 General Grant gave General Sherman command of the Shenandoah Army and he conducted a campaign of systematic devastation in the valley, destroying it as a base for Confederate operations and supplies.

dedicated, well-armed armies dug in and faced each other across a shell-ravaged no-man's-land. Neither could break the other's defenses and every attempt to do so was a costly failure. Grant sat in front of Petersburg for nine months but fortress Virginia stood alone. Elsewhere the Confederacy was collapsing in ruins as Sherman left Atlanta and burned and destroyed his way through Georgia towards the sea before turning north in a series of lightning campaigns that shattered army after army. Robert E. Lee remained pinned down at Petersburg as Grant built up the forces to overrun him, and General Philip Sheridan marched his Army of the Shenandoah across Virginia to attack his right flank. During the night of April 2, 1865, Lee withdrew from the trenches of Petersburg, leaving the road to Richmond open to the Union. The war had just another week to run.

Visitors to the small town of Appomattox today may tour a reconstructed Meeks General Store, Woodson Law Office and County Jail. They may visit the rebuilt McLean House where Lee met Grant on April 9, 1865. With Grant chasing him from behind and cut off to the west and south by Sheridan, Lee asked for a meeting. In full dress uniform, Lee sat down with Grant in McLean's living room and signed the surrender. When the Union troops outside began to cheer, Grant ordered them to stop, saying: "The war is over; the rebels are our countrymen again".

*Above* His president, Abraham Lincoln, portrayed by Matthew Wilson.

*Left* Lee eventually surrendered at the McLean House. The Civil War had swept back and forth across Virginia soil for nearly four years, Lee mostly defending the Confederacy, despite inferior numbers and supplies, with consummate brilliance. Sherman's campaign of destruction in Georgia, the weight of Northern forces, and the withering effect of the siege of Petersburg eventually forced Lee's surrender.

*Above* The surrender of Robert E. Lee to
General Ulysses S. Grant, April 9 1865, in the
house of Wilmer McLean. Grant himself
wrote the liberal surrender terms, and ordered
the Union cheering which greeted Lee's
departure to cease. The surrender site is now
in the Appomattox Court House National
Historical Park, and you can see the actual
spot where the men laid down their arms.

*Right* Robert E. Lee was born into the
aristocratic Virginian clan of the Lees, and was
educated at Alexandria Academy and West
Point. He served with distinction in the
Mexican War and commanded the units
which suppressed the uprising at Harper's
Ferry. A Unionist and a critic of slavery, he
nevertheless decided at the outbreak of the
Civil War that his true loyalties lay with the
state of Virginia.

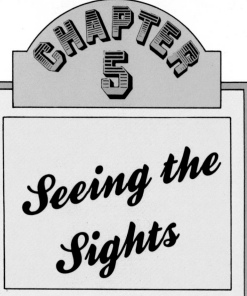
# Seeing the Sights

South of Washington, DC, US Interstate 95 takes you directly through Fredericksburg to Richmond. If you leave Washington during the rush hour you will sympathize with Thomas Jefferson, who once complained that he "could never go more than three miles an hour" – it was the primitive condition of the roads that caused the delay then, of course, not congestion! Just before crossing the Potomac, you will pass the Jefferson Memorial. The highway to Fredericksburg follows part of the route taken by the Union Army advancing on Richmond, but the residents are far friendlier now.

The Fredericksburg and Spotsylvania National Park covers some 3500 acres and contains four major Civil War battlefields, including Chancellorsville and Fredericksburg. Markers show battle positions and entrenched fortifications, and this pleasant landscape wears a sadness which belongs only to old silent battlefields. In Fredericksburg itself, colonial buffs may visit the James Monroe Museum and Memorial Library, in the building in which Monroe practiced law in the 1780s. The museum has the Louis XVI desk on which he wrote the Monroe Doctrine. The town also has an apothecary shop with rooms George Washington used when he visited Fredericksburg, as well as the house he built for his mother.

Richmond, the state capital, is a blend of industrialized city and historic grandeur. This once-proud capital of the Confederate States of America hosts its own Civil War Battlefield National Park,

*Left* This Fourth of July float carries the products of one of the many old crafts to have survived. The quilts were made by a cooperative of mountain women.

and one can make a tour of nearly 60 miles of old trench lines and battle lines. Any devotee of early American history must visit the Capitol building, designed by Thomas Jefferson, St John's Church, where Patrick Henry made his fiery "give me liberty, or give me death" call to the Virginia Convention, and the John Marshall House, built around 1790. Appointed Chief Justice of the Supreme Court in 1801, Marshall had the distinction of being one of Thomas Jefferson's chief political enemies and – more importantly for America's future – the jurist who established the judiciary's right to overturn Acts of Congress it ruled to be unconstitutional. From then on, America's government was officially one where law was paramount.

Richmond's Valentine Museum (East Clay Street) is for the historically minded, and for the artistic there is the Virginia Museum of Fine Arts (Grove Avenue and Boulevard). Readers of American literature will not want to miss the Old Stone House, which is now a memorial museum to Edgar Allan Poe, who worked as an editor and writer in Richmond for several years. Poe's mother is buried in St John's Churchyard.

Sixty miles west of Richmond is the area of Charlottesville. Here is the University of Virginia, founded and planned by Thomas Jefferson – he considered this and the Declaration of Independence to be his chief contributions to the country – and, of course, Monticello, the 35-room mansion he devoted his life to creating. Nearby is Ash Lawn, another colonial estate, the home of Jefferson's friend James Monroe. The Michie Tavern Museum is also close to Monticello and, as an eighteenth-century inn, hosted both Jefferson and Monroe. Another famous guest was the French General Lafayette, Washington's staunch ally during the Revolutionary War. The tavern is still a versatile restaurant, but it is also now an extensive museum.

Driving south from Richmond on US 95 takes us close to Petersburg (it's a short hop west on US 85), where the South finally lost the Civil War. One of the highlights of a tour of the Petersburg National Battlefield Park is the crater (170 feet by 60 feet, and 30 feet deep) blasted in July 1864, when Union soldiers tunneled 510 feet and exploded 4 tons of powder under Confederate lines. The explosion blew a huge hole in Lee's trenches and killed nearly 300 people.

Driving east from Richmond on US 64 is a journey back in time to Williamsburg, where one experiences a quiet, modern city understandably in love with its past. Yearly spring-to-fall demonstrations of colonial military drill with a local militia in full costume are colorful and exciting

*Left* An aerial view of the Blue Ridge, near Elkton – the view of its entire length is a quiet composition of sky and horizon, with one secluded valley after another. Governor Spotswood and his Knights of the Golden Horseshoe reached the peak of the Blue Ridge in 1716.

*Above* The Shenandoah Valley lies between the Blue Ridge Mountains and the Alleghenies and is watered by the Shenandoah River to the north and the New River to the south. Rather than the normal American east-west frontier pattern, the valley was populated from the north, by German and Scotch-Irish immigrants.

*Right* Natural Bridge crosses a 215-foot gorge cut by Cedar Creek from the limestone rock. George Washington carved his initials 23 feet up one wall, and Thomas Jefferson bought it from George III for 20 shillings. During the Revolution it was used as a shot tower to make bullets for the American army.

*Above* A statue of James Monroe, fifth President of the United States of America, at his Ash Lawn home near Charlottesville, not far from Jefferson's Monticello. Jefferson helped to plan Ash Lawn, a frame house with a boxwood garden. This statue is an impressive 16 feet high.

reminders of Williamsburg's former prominence. Once the social, political and cultural capital of Virginia, Williamsburg has the world's largest number of reconstructed eighteenth-century buildings. There is a variety of operating colonial crafts shops, including blacksmiths, wigmakers, bookbinders, bakeries, cabinet makers and silversmiths.

Lovers of historic mysteries shouldn't miss Williamsburg's Wythe House. Signer of the Declaration of Independence and teacher of Thomas Jefferson, Patrick Henry and John Marshall, Wythe was one of colonial Virginia's leading figures. When Wythe was in his eighties, someone put arsenic in his tea, but the murderer was never caught.

Other reconstructions include the Governor's Palace (besides Britain's colonial governors, Jefferson and Patrick Henry used it before the new state of Virginia moved its capital to Richmond) and gardens. William and Mary College, the second-oldest institution of higher learning in America, boasts Presidents Jefferson, Monroe and Tyler as graduates, as well as the Christopher Wren building, built in 1695 and probably the oldest academic building in America.

Stately plantation houses lie on State Highway 5, which runs between Williamsburg and Richmond. There is President Tyler's Sherwood Forest, and Berkeley, the Harrison family home. Belle Air, Evelynton and Westover are mansions associated with the Byrd family. William Byrd II, builder of the Westover that stands today, died in 1744, the very model of a wealthy Virginia landowner and gentleman scholar. His son committed suicide after wasting his fortune, and the family faded from prominence until the early part of this century, when Senator Harry F. Byrd ruled the Virginia Democratic Party for years and became one of Washington's king-makers. His fame was matched locally by his brother Thomas, who built a highly profitable apple industry in the Shenandoah Valley, but was surpassed nationally by another brother, Richard, who was the first man to fly over the South Pole (in 1928), just after establishing the Polar exploration base "Little America".

Both Jamestown and Yorktown are a short drive from Williamsburg. In Jamestown there is the old Church Tower built in 1639, foundations of many of the original buildings, a seventeenth-century-style center for colonial glass-blowing,

*Above* Fort Monroe, Hampton, built between 1819 and 1834, is the largest stone fort in America. Its moat is 8 feet deep and 60 to 150 feet wide. In the Civil War it was one of the few forts not captured by the South, and the battle between the *Monitor* and the *Merrimack* was part of a Confederate plan to destroy the Union navy in Hampton Roads and starve the fort out.

*Facing page, top* Thomas Jefferson's Rotunda and Lawn at his University of Virginia, Charlottesville is put to good use: here, an open-air concert by the Glee Club given on a Sunday afternoon in May – a new use for a lovely old building.

and, moored on the river, full-sized replicas of the three little ships which brought the first English settlers to Jamestown in 1607. Nearby there are archeological excavations at Martin's Hundred, one of Virginia's first plantations, wiped out in the Indian raid of 1622. Diggings at the site have shown a pattern of early colonial life that was far more tied to the economy of Europe than anyone had previously believed.

Further east on US 66 lies Hampton, with its Fort Monroe, the oldest stone-built fort in America; surrounded by a wide moat, it once held prisoner Jefferson Davis, former President of the Confederacy. As a complete contrast, three miles north of Hampton is NASA's Langley Research Center, which was vitally involved with the Mercury and Viking projects. Among many other exhibits, its visitor center has the Apollo 12 spacecraft, moon rock and Alan Shepard's space suit. Today, Langley works on the space shuttle, among other things.

Leaving Hampton to the southeast takes you across the inner end of Chesapeake Bay via the Hampton Roads Bridge Tunnel to Norfolk and the end of US 66. Norfolk has the brashness that

comes with hosting the world's largest naval base, being the headquarters for the Atlantic Fleet. With nearby Plymouth, it makes up one of the oldest naval facilities in America. It is the home of the Chrysler Art Museum, one of the finest of its kind in the United States. A Norfolk courthouse built in the 1850s has been turned into a memorial museum for General Douglas MacArthur, conqueror of Japan in World War II and generally thought one of the world's most brilliant military leaders. The General's crypt is set into the floor of the rotunda.

Not far away is Virginia Beach, one of the East Coast's most popular seaside resorts. It is the world's longest beach resort city (45 km) and is the site of the Atlantic Coast's surfing championships held each July.

Fifteen miles south of Washington, DC is Alexandria and Mount Vernon, the plantation home of the first President, George Washington. In Alexandria, Gadsby's Tavern (North Royal Street) was patronized by Washington, and it has been fully restored as a museum and restaurant. He also attended services at nearby Christ Church (as did Robert E. Lee). Mount Vernon was Washington's estate and burial place, and in addition to

*Above* Music is an important part of the cultural life of Virginia, especially in the Highlands, and the banjo is *the* instrument for Virginian mountain music.

the unique and beautiful mid-Georgian mansion there are 30 acres of exhibition area to see. South of Mount Vernon is Gunston Hall, built in 1755 by George Mason, father of the Bill of Rights. Just across the Potomac from Washington, DC is the suburb of Arlington, home to both the Pentagon and America's most famous cemetery. Among the many people buried there are John Fitzgerald Kennedy and his brother Robert. At the north end is the Marine Memorial, a 78-foot bronze statue representing the raising of the flag on Iwo Jima in 1945. Overlooking Arlington Cemetery is the former home of Robert E. Lee.

Running down western Virginia are the Blue Ridge Mountains and beyond them the Shenandoah Valley – the name "Shenandoah" comes from an Indian word meaning "Daughter of the Stars". Skyline Drive along the crest of the Blue Ridge Mountains in Shenandoah National Park offers some of America's most spectacular scenery, and spring finds people coming from all over to see the azaleas and rhododendrons in bloom. There is abundant wildlife, including some black bear, wild turkey, and elk imported from Wyoming. Much of the folk music from this area has become rooted in American culture. The town of Bristol, right on the border with Tennessee, considers itself to be the wellspring of country and bluegrass music, and each May there is the fiercely competitive music festival known as Appalachian Music Days.

At the top of the Shenandoah Valley is Winchester, where the young George Washington worked as a surveyor. His former base office on Cork and Braddock Streets is now a museum. Winchester is also host to a yearly Apple Blossom Festival – Frederick County alone has 700 000 apple trees! Washington and Lee University is at Lexington; in the Chapel is the crypt of Robert E. Lee and his family. Nearby is the Virginia Military Institute, which is renowned for producing famous generals and is the site of the George C. Marshall Library.

Marshall, a graduate of the Institute, was Eisenhower's commander as US Chief of Staff in World War II. After the war, he served as Secretary of State and was the architect of the Marshall Plan, aimed at reconstructing Western Europe. The Institute also holds mementos of another of its famous graduates, General George S. "Old-Blood-and-Guts" Patton, whose US Third Army crossed France and Southern Germany after D-Day.

*Right* A traditional way of having fun: the women in their full-skirted dresses twirl round to the rhythms of Appalachian square-dancing music. The music and dancing have their roots deep in the social and cultural history of Virginia.

*Below* Albert Hash, Flurry Doe and Emily and Thornton Spencer. Bristol boasts of being the birthplace of country music and in its annual festival, Appalachian Music Days, cash prizes for bluegrass and country music performances are awarded.

*Above* Part of the plentiful wildlife of the Shenandoah Valley, the elk (*Cervus canadensis*) was imported from Wyoming. A member of the deer family, second only in size to the moose, it is one of North America's largest herbivores.

*Left* This magnificent, if somewhat bad-tempered-looking specimen, is a male North American wild turkey (*Meleagris golloparvo*). Misnamed because it was believed that it came from Turkey, the bird was a welcome discovery for the pioneer colonists of North America.

*Right* This splendid creature, the black bear, is also found in the Shenandoah Valley. Treat him with respect, even if you do think he looks cuddly – he is not someone to mess around with. He enjoys a varied diet, and is one of the largest carnivores in the world.

*Above* The Virginian Military Institute treasures many items in memorial of Stonewall Jackson, George C. Patton and the battle of New Market as well as other objects illuminating the military traditions of the Institute. The Hall has the renowned Clindinst mural depicting the cadets at the battle of New Market.

*Left* Exhibits in the visitor center at the National Aeronautics and Space Administration Langley Research Center, the country's oldest aviation research facility, founded in 1917. The center played a key part in aircraft streamlining, and more recently in the Mercury and Viking Projects.

*Facing page, top* The Pentagon derives its name from its shape – blocks forming a five-sided unit. The nerve center of the Defense Department and the military as a whole, it continues the traditional involvement of Virginia with the armed forces, and is an important large employer of Virginian people.

*Facing page, bottom* The solemn and dignified last resting place of John F. Kennedy (1917-63), President of the United States, assassinated in his prime in Dallas. Since then, security arrangements for Presidents are even more stringent, but complete safety can never be guaranteed.

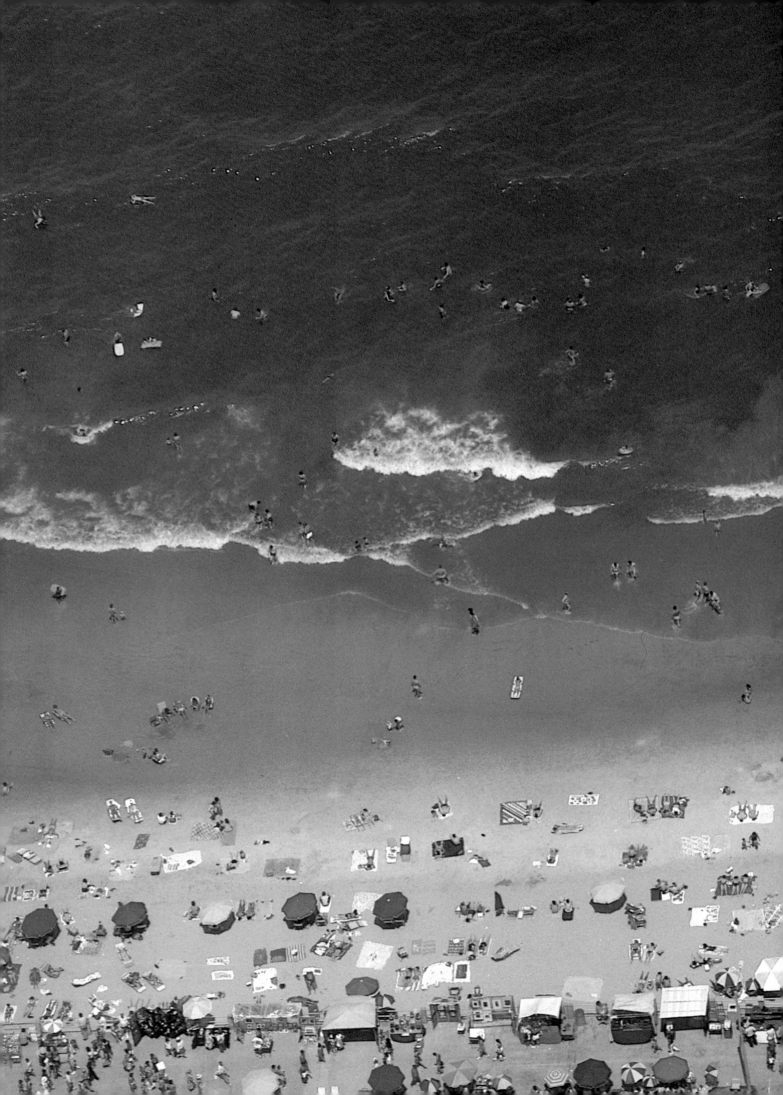

# CHAPTER 6

## Modern Days

The Virginia of today is youthful, dynamic, open; the speed and intensity of change over the past four or five decades has radically transformed the face of the state, urbanizing large parts of it in just a few short years. Today, northern Virginia is the southernmost end of a vast megalopolis sprawling down the Eastern Seaboard from Washington, DC and then on to Richmond. More than half of Virginians now live in cities – apart from the northern counties and Richmond, Norfolk and Plymouth form a bustling metropolis, and there are smaller but growing cities scattered right across the state.

No longer in the grip of a single industry – tobacco – Virginia's economy has diversified at astonishing speed. Agriculture has remained vital, but industry has boomed, providing a broad variety of jobs for the younger generation. It has become a major center of manufacturing, making textiles, apparel, chemicals, books, furniture, and so on. Recruitment from abroad has been extremely successful; the state has attracted important plants from Sweden (Volvo – the first US assembly plant of a foreign auto maker), France, West Germany, and Switzerland. Its fine harbor potential in the Hampton Roads area has drawn in a fantastic array of military facilities, and the Newport News Shipbuilding and Drydock Company, one of the largest privately owned shipyards in the world, has built vessels ranging from tugs and passenger liners to aircraft carriers and Polaris submarines. The populace welcomes the activity of the

*Left* Part of the stunning sweep of Virginia Beach's fine 12-mile public beach. Hugely popular, it caters for almost any recreation.

military, because every year the Defense Department spends no less than $1.2 billion. In addition to this there are NASA expenditures of more than $125 million a year. Research is a vital activity: often at the forefront of technology, the state has the research facilities of several national blue-chip companies; Virginia was the site of the nation's first *in vitro* fertilization clinic, and the birth of the USA's first "test tube baby" took place there; and a rocket fired from NASA's Wallops Island rocket-launching base enabled Dr James Van Allen to discover the layers of intense radiation surrounding the Earth which now bear his name.

Despite all this urbanization, modernization, diversification and high tech, there is in Virginians a proud consciousness of the distinguished past of their state. The careful preservation and reconstruction of physical reminders testify eloquently to the importance Virginians attach to their heritage. In north Virginia, it is not far from plantations to skyscrapers – towns like Alexandria have both. In Tidewater, it is not far from colonial Williamsburg to NASA's Langley Research Center. As well as the tangible remains of the past, there are festivals, re-enactments and dramas which keep alive the memory of bygone days – the Abingdon Virginia Highlands Festival, for instance, or Winchester's Apple Blossom Festival, or Yorktown Day. As Douglas Southall Freeman said: "Life is more leisured . . . There is a deliberate cult of the past."

Although there have been many changes, some things are still the same. Traditional rural life remains, and west of the Blue Ridge Mountains historic patterns of small family farms and stoutly independent lifestyle are much as they were. The mountain folk of the Blue Ridge Mountains, where the pioneering spirit still lives on, have preserved old ways more than most people: a dialect close to Elizabethan English lingered among them until this century, and, perhaps even closer to their hearts, the tradition of moonshine! Franklin County is still one of the great moonshining counties of America. (Recently, revenue agents seized as many as 424 illicit stills in Virginia in a single year, and disposed of 23 000 gallons of moonshine.) And although tobacco is, as we have seen, no longer the dominating influence it once was, the colorful and bustling tobacco auctions of Danville still earn the place the title of the World's Best Tobacco Market. It is an aromatic and entertaining tradition with some of the world's foremost

*Above* Despite the huge growth industry and high technology over the past few decades, this idyllic rural scene, with its traditional barn surrounded by cattle and sheep, emphasizes the continuing importance of agriculture.

*Right* From the very beginnings of the colony, turkeys have played their vital part. Poultry has for long been an important element of the Virginian economy, and turkeys are still farmed on a large scale, as this scene clearly demonstrates!

*Facing page* Despite the high technology of much of Virginia's agricultural industry, some farming is still done by age-old traditional methods – here we see the hand-planting of seeds, a back-breaking exercise.

(and fastest!) auctioneering talents working in eighteen warehouses, which all ring with the urgent bidding. As if to illustrate the Virginia mixture of modern industry and historical survivals, Danville also boasts the largest single-unit textile mill in the world.

So although Virginia is a rapidly growing area, its character, its essential vitality, and its pride in its past have not changed. Despite the swift pace of development, many things have remained constant. The breathtaking exuberance of today mingles with the timeless grace of yesteryear. To be *born* a Virginian is a special mark of favor in the Old Dominion. The days of aristocratic society and gracious (for the owners) plantation lives may be over, but respect for the past and for ancestors lives on.

And Supersonic jets may roar off from the ultra-modern Dulles International Airport for destinations all over the world, but chances are that they will hardly disturb the romance of the Shenandoah Valley:

> *O Shenandoah, I long to hear you,*
> *Away, you rolling river.*
> *O Shenandoah, I long to hear you,*
> *Away I'm bound away,*
> *'Cross the wide Missouri.*

*Left* This sensuous, sumptuous scene shows the variety and colorfulness of Virginia's vegetable and fruit produce.

*Facing page, top* In the tradition of good neighborliness and friendliness, Virginians can always drop in for a chat and to find out the latest news at their local store.

*Facing page, bottom* Time-honored customs are still observed in Virginia: this boy is selling pumpkins for halloween near Stuart, Virginia.

*Left* An early stage in producing the crop most closely associated with Virginia – tobacco. The young plants need skilled handling – not everything can be done by machine!

*Below* From the small seedlings the tobacco plants grow to the size of these, hung up to dry in a barn mouth in Wilson, Virginia. Between August and November the processing of the leaf takes place, a busy and bustling time.

*Right* Although tobacco is no longer of the central importance it once was, in parts of south and central Virginia it is still the big money crop. The tobacco shown here would eventually find its way to an auction like those in Danville.

*Facing page, top* A coal carman watches for the next wagons. The relatively limited coal industry region of western Virginia is often called the "triangular wedge." The Highlands have some industry, but the most important income comes from coal.

*Facing page, bottom* This is the coal supply for Clinch River Power Plant – obviously a hungry consumer. The traditional source of power fuels the production of energy for the most modern high technology industries.

*Right* Although much of the industry is now mechanized and automated, coal miners are still necessary. Coal mining provides a payroll of over $100 million, and without it employment prospects for typical Appalachian folk might be even worse than they are now.

*Below* Coal pours into wagons in Wise County. Virginian coal production doubled in the 1970s, and the state now produces about 6 per cent of US coal, although the industry has also felt the pinch of world recession.

*Facing page* Wild ponies along the shore of Chincoteague Island. There is an annual Chincoteague Pony-Penning Carnival in which the wild ponies, rumored to be descendants of horses which swam ashore from a wrecked Spanish galleon in the sixteenth century, are herded together and sold for the benefit of local firemen.

*Right* A vivid reminder of the Old World, foxhunters pursue their prey in the traditional British costume. Just up ahead, no doubt, are the traditional British foxhounds. Northern Virginia particularly is horse country and hosts the oldest and liveliest hunts in America.

*Below* Montpelier, a large Greek Revival mansion four miles west of Orange, was once the home of James Madison. It is now private, but in the fall the Montpelier Races are held in its grounds. The events include brush, hurdle and flat races.

*Facing page, top* Despite its up-to-the-minute, skyscraper appearance, Richmond's history dates back to 1737 when it was founded on the banks of the James River.

*Facing page, bottom* The Rotunda, Tyson's corner – modern grace and harmony or intimidating by its sheer scale?

*Right* The Virginian Museum of Fine Arts has a marvelous collection of Fabergé jewelry, a marble statue of Caligula and a fine gallery of Art Nouveau works.

*Below* As well as being the center of trade and part of the world's largest naval base, Norfolk still has plenty to offer the historically minded.

*Above* Most of the men on Tangier Island, Chesapeake Bay are fishermen. Settled in the late 1600s, the Island keeps up many of the old customs, and the inhabitants still have a flavor of the Elizabethan in their voices. Many claim descent from the original families.

*Left* Virginia Beach is renowned for its fine long sandy beach and offers superb fishing, surfing, swimming, amusement park jollity and exclusive nightclubbing – or you can just laze about on the beach!

*Facing page* One of the more modern (and breathtaking) attractions of Busch Gardens, "The Old Country" theme park just near Williamsburg. The park also has recreations of English, French, German and Italian villages of the eighteenth-century.

# Things to see in Virginia

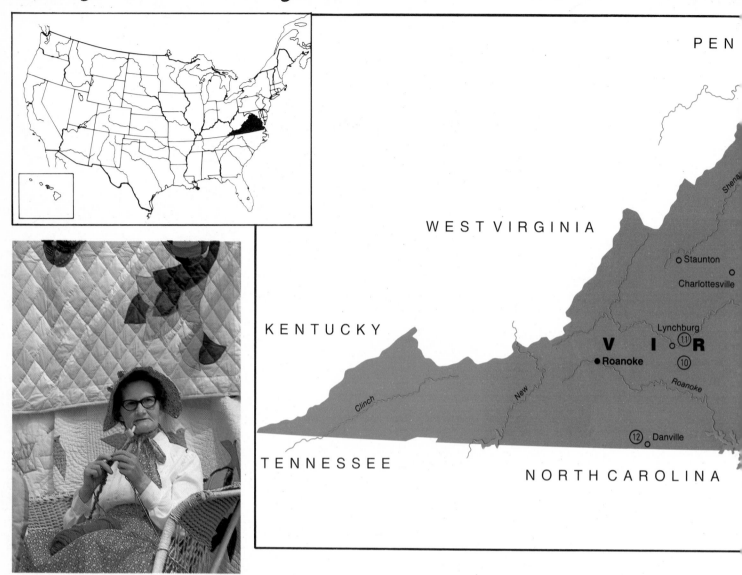

PEN

WEST VIRGINIA

KENTUCKY

TENNESSEE

NORTH CAROLINA

o Staunton
Charlottesville

Lynchburg
V I R
(11)
● Roanoke (10)

Roanoke

(12) o Danville

Shena
Clinch
New

**1 Jamestown** was the first English colony in Virginia, founded in 1607 when three tiny ships landed 120 bold colonists sent by Queen Elizabeth's favorite courtier, Sir Walter Raleigh.

**2** Once the center of cultural life in the colony, **Williamsburg** now has an impressive area of reconstructed and restored eighteenth-century buildings.

**3** George Washington was devoted to his plantation home, **Mount Vernon,** which is still a working farm. The gardens and grounds are much as the first President left them.

**4** The third President, Thomas Jefferson, leveled a 857-foot mountaintop to build **Monticello,** a unique classical-style home.

**5** The British General Cornwallis surrendered at **Yorktown** at the end of the War of Independence. At the Victory Center you can trace the Revolution from Bunker Hill to Yorktown.

**6** Today a busy commercial center, **Alexandria** was an important cultural and political center in the eighteenth-century. George Washington had a house there. In Old Town Alexandria cobbled streets run between beautiful eighteenth-century houses.

**7** This huge naval base, **Norfolk,** home port of the Atlantic Fleet, is a major industrial, military and trade center. It has many points of historical interest, including the Hermitage Foundation Museum in a Tudor-style country house.

**8** On the banks of the James river, **Richmond** was the capital of the Confederacy during the Civil War. Among many points of interest are the Capitol, designed by Thomas Jefferson, and the house of Jefferson Davis, President of the Confederacy.

**9** In **Fredericksburg and Spotsylvania National Military Park** four battlefields – Fredericksburg, Chancellorsville, the Wilderness and Spotsylvania Court House – are remembered in an area of some 6500 acres.

**10** Today, the preserved village of **Appomattox Court House** looks much as it did when Robert E. Lee surrendered there at the end of the Civil War. The McLean House, where General Grant wrote the surrender terms, and Surrender Triangle, where Confederate troops laid down their arms, are particularly poignant spots.

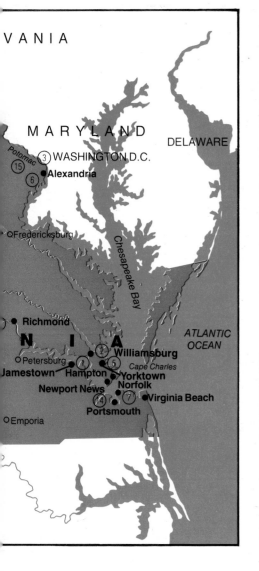

**11** Built in the early nineteenth-century, **Fort Monroe** is a huge stone-built, star-shaped fort, surrounded by a deep wide moat. Jefferson Davis was held prisoner here for a while.

**12** Now a fascinating mix of modern and historic, **Danville** was where Jefferson Davis saw out the last days of the Civil War. Its tobacco auctions are lively, intriguing scenes.

**13** The **Shenandoah Valley** was for a long time frontier land, and even today, with its German and Scotch-Irish influences, it is still distinctive. Its natural beauties vie with the interest of its traditional way of life.

**14** For devotees of more recent, technological history, the visitor center at the **National Aeronautics and Space Administration Langley Research Center** is a must.

**15** Across the Potomac River from Washington, DC is the most renowned of America's national cemeteries, **Arlington.** About 176 000 people are buried here, both the illustrious and the unknown.

## PICTURE CREDITS

POWHATAN

Held this state & fashion when Capt. Smith was deliuered to him prisoner

MONACANS

Monahassanugh
Rassawek
Monasukapanough

Massinacack

Mowhemcho

Stegara
Shackaconia

MAN

PI

The Fales

Powhatan

Arrohatteck
Orapaks
Cattachiptico
Passaunkack
Utcustank
Accoquek
Secobeck
Anaskenoans

POWH A TAN

Appamatuck

Nechanicoke

Apocant

Quackcobowan

Mayvmkuspin

Martoughquaunk
Muttamussinsack
Chesapiooc
Nandtaughtacund
Anemapeugah

MAN

Attanoughkomouck

Weanock
Paspaheigh
Quackcowean

Attamtuck
Potauncae

Accossiwinck

Kupkipcock

Kerahocak

GOAGS

Moyse
Acconc

Tsenacomacah
Vttamussah
Menascucten
Matchut

Pissaseck

CHA

Chawope

Werawahon
Orenock

Oquogheton

Chiskiack
Mamanahunt
Anguteck
Mamanahunt
Payankatank

Nawacaten
Mangoraca
Wecuppom
Matchopick
Poruptanck
Paspatanzy

WONS

Nantapoyac
Mattapament

Pasaughtacock

Cuttatawomen

Powcomonet

Jamestowne
Mattacock
Mathomauk
Weroucomoco
Werowocomoco

Warraskoyack
Mokete

Opiscopank
Cantaunkack

Peyankatank
Menaskunt

Teracoseck
Nandfamund
Mattanock

Kishkiack
Ceader Ile
Capahowosick
Parankatank

Cekakawwon

Shapes Ile
Manteoughquemec
Ceader Ile
Gosnolds bay
Kandals poynt

Iffins poynt
Point Warde

KVS

Chesapeack
Ritfons point bay

Powhatan Flu
Poynt comfort
ILE
Ruffels Iles

Cape Henry

Mortons baye

Cape Charles
Accowmack
Accomack
Keales Ile
Roules poynt
Wighcocomoco
Smyths Iles

THE

VIRGINIAN SEA